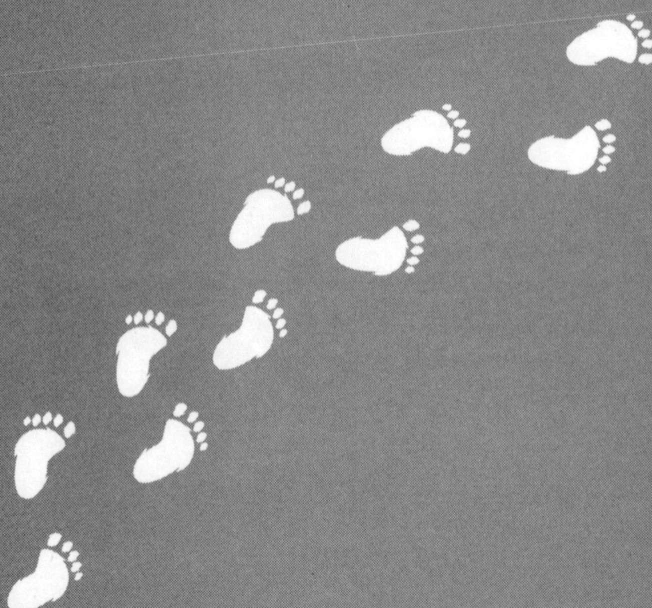

Hairy Holes

This is a Magabala Book
LEADING PUBLISHER OF ABORIGINAL AND
TORRES STRAIT ISLANDER STORYTELLERS.
CHANGING THE WORLD, ONE STORY AT A TIME.

First published 2023
Magabala Books Aboriginal Corporation
1 Bagot Street, Broome, Western Australia
Website: www.magabala.com
Email: sales@magabala.com

Magabala Books receives financial assistance from the Commonwealth Government through the Australia Council, its arts advisory body. The State of Western Australia has made an investment in this project through the Department of Local Government, Sport and Cultural Industries. Magabala Books would like to acknowledge the generous support of the Shire of Broome, Western Australia.

Magabala Books is Australia's only independent Aboriginal and Torres Strait Islander publishing house. Magabala Books acknowledges the Traditional Owners of the Country on which we live and work. We recognise the unbroken connection to traditional lands, waters and cultures. Through what we publish, we honour all our Elders, peoples and stories, past, present and future.

Cover and Internal Design by Jo Hunt
Printed and bound by Griffin Press, South Australia

ISBN (Print) 978-1-922613-18-9
ISBN (ePUB) 978-1-922613-17-2

NATIONAL LIBRARY OF AUSTRALIA
A catalogue record for this book is available from the National Library of Australia

Department of Local Government, Sport and Cultural Industries
GOVERNMENT OF WESTERN AUSTRALIA
lotterywest supported
Shire of Broome people · place · prosperity
Australian Government
Australia Council for the Arts

BRENTON E MCKENNA

Hairy Holes

Magabala Books

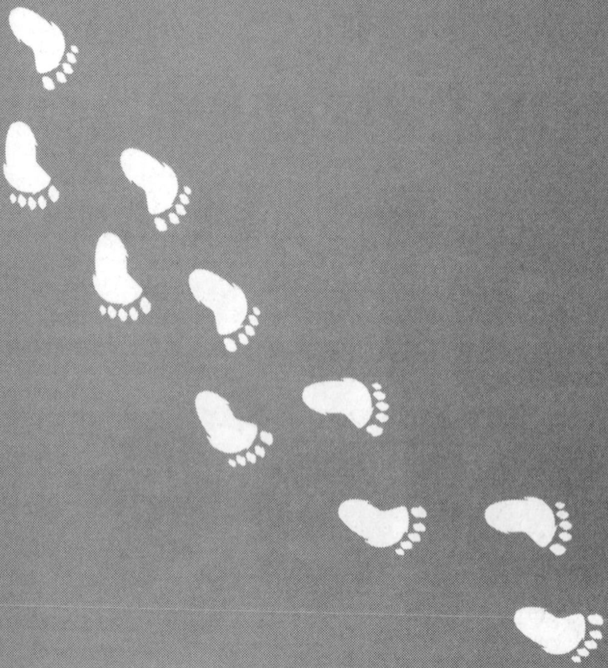

1967
NEPAL
COMPARISON
PRIMATE SKELETON
OUR HISTORY IS FULL OF STORIES ABOUT HAIRY PEOPLE, FURRY PEOPLE, YOWIES, BUNYIPS & MONSTER APES.
BUT THIS IS A STORY ABOUT THE HAIRY HOLERS.
THEY'RE LIKE THE WEIRD COUSINS OF HAIRY PEOPLE. THEY KEPT TO THEMSELVES A LOT.
UNTIL THE NEW PEOPLE CAME.

THE NEW PEOPLE WENT TO WAR WITH THE OLD PEOPLE.

THE NEW PEOPLE STARTED EATING EVERYTHING, DESTROYING THE SACRED BALANCE.

SO THE HAIRY HOLERS THOUGHT IT WOULD BE A GOOD IDEA,
TO EAT SOME OF THE NEW PEOPLE.
TURNS OUT IT WAS A BAD IDEA.
A VERY BAD IDEA

15 YEARS AGO

YO LADY! PULL OVER AND POP A SQUAT. I JUST SAW SOMETHING KRAY-ZAY!
DON'T YOU DARE CALL ME LADY. I AM YOUR MOTHER, YOUNG MAN!!
NO. WEK
AH C'MON LAD... I MEAN MUM.

THE OUTBACK.
BEAUTIFUL.
MAJESTIC.

AND JUST...
PLAIN SCARY!!
GGGRRROOOOOOWWWWLLL!!

GGGGRRRRRGGGGRRRRR!!!
GGGRRRGGGGGRRRRGGGRRRR!!!

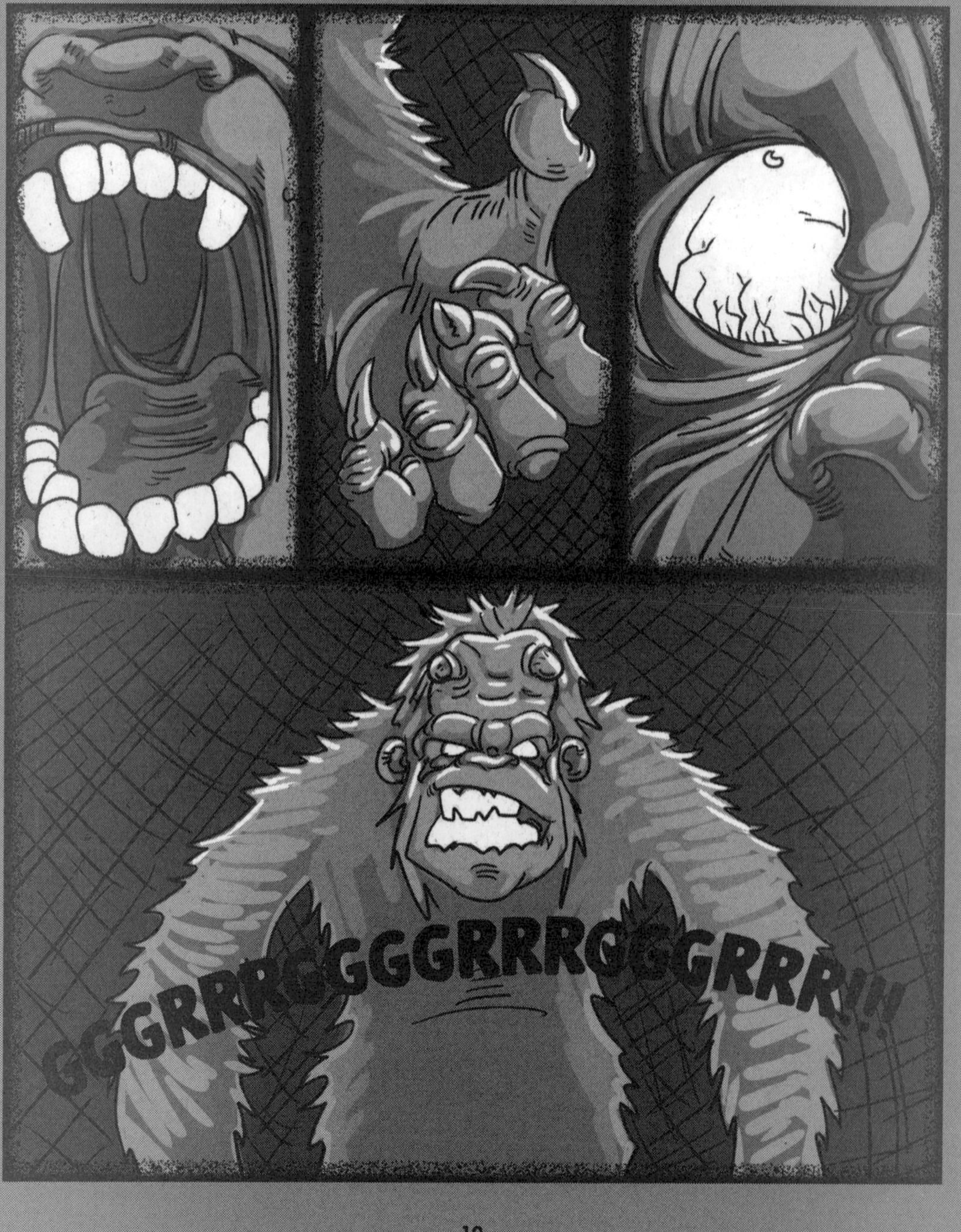
GGGRRRRGGGGRRRRGGGRRRR!!!

GAAAOOOO!!!!

GOOD
MORNING

One

GOOD MORNING, DEAD BULL SKULL.
GOOD MORNING, NEST OF MULGA SNAKES.
GOOD MORNING, WILD DINGOES.
GOOD MORNING, BOULDER SHAPED LIKE ELVIS.

GOOD MORNING OUTBACK!
IT'S GOING TO BE A WONDERFUL DAY!

SHUT! YOUR! HOLE!!
WE GET IT! IT'S MORNING TIME!
REDLEY HOLE A.K.A RED HOLE.
GOOD MORNING... REDLEY.
I'M OUTTA GRUB TEA.
THIS IS BEGLEY HOLE A.K.A BEG HOLE.

SORRY FOR WAKING YOU UP, REDLEY.
WHERE ARE ALL THE GRUBS? I SAW HEAPS BEFORE.
BUT I BELIEVE IT'S IMPORTANT TO SAY GOOD MORNING TO EVERYONE YOU MEET, EVERYDAY.
TICK! TICK! TICK!
SNAP!

LOOK AROUND YOU! NUMBNUT. DON'T BE EXPECTING A RETURN GREETING ANYTIME SOON.

BECAUSE WE IN THE FREAKIN' DESERT!!!

NOTHING SAYS 'GOOD MORNING' HERE, BECAUSE EVERYTHING IS HOT, MISERABLE AND TRYIN' TO KILL YOU!!
REDLEY!
ONLY SKINNIES SAY 'GOOD MORNING', WE DON'T LIKE SKINNIES! WE EAT THEM.
REDLEY!
SKINNIES: REDLEY'S TERM FOR HUMANS SINCE THEY ARE COVERED IN SKIN.
REDLEY!
ONLY THING THAT LOOKS REMOTELY HAPPY OUT HERE OTHER THAN YOU...
IS THAT STUPID ROCK THAT LOOKS LIKE ELVIS.

RED!
WHAT!!
LOOK! OVER THERE!

SCRUNCH!
SCRUNCH!
SCRUNCH!
SCRUNCH!
SCRUNCH!
SCRUNCH!

NONE OF THIS LOOKS FAMILIAR. DOESN'T LOOK LIKE ADELAIDE AT ALL.
MAYBE THE MAP'S UPSIDE DOWN.
SCRAK!
OOOFF!!
WHAT THE..? WHERE DID THIS WALL OF FUR COME FROM?

AH...AH...HEL...LO.
GOOD MORNING!
IDIOT.

UH-OH!
THUD!
I THINK I KILLED HIM.
BUZZ
BUZZ
GOOD!
LET'S EAT HIM.

Two

HUH!
AAAHHHH!!
OMG! WTH!
BUGGER!
SEE, TOLD YOU HE WASN'T DEAD.

NO SKINNY STEAK TONIGHT.
WAS LOOKIN' FORWARD TO EATING SOME SKINNY STEAKS.
OUCH!!!
Y'KNOW, FOR A SKINNY, HE'S KINDA SKINNY.
WHAT! YOU CAN TALK! WHAT'S A SKINNY?
NO! STAY AWAY FROM ME!!!

RELAX BUDDY, YOU'RE OK. NOBODY IS EATING SKINNY STEAKS ANYTIME SOON.
PFFT! ... SAYS YOU!
WHO...WHO... WHAT ARE YOU? ARE YOU REAL OR AM I DREAMING?
YEAH, I'M REAL, MATE.
YEAH, REAL YARM!
YARM: CLUMSY

MY NAME'S BEGLEY AND THIS IS MY BROTHER REDLEY.
YOU ARE YOWIE!
A WHAT?
WE NOT YOWIES, WE HAIRY HOLERS.
THIS SKINNY, HE NOT RIGHT! HE LOOK AND SMELL FUNNY. HE MIGHT BE SINGING US.
NO! NO I CAN'T SING TO SAVE MY LIFE. ALL I'M SAYING IS THAT YOU LOOK LIKE A YOWIE.
JUST LET ME EXPLAIN.

MY NAME IS JOPLIN AND I'M A COMPUTER PROGRAMMER.
LOOK, HERE IS MY LITTLE MAGIC BOX WITH PRETTY LITTLE LIGHTS CALLED A 'LAPTOP'.
WITH THIS 'LAPTOP' I'M GOING TO SEARCH IMAGES OF A SASQUATCH.
THAT WAY YOU KNOW I'M NOT LAUGHING OR 'SINGING ' AT YOU. I MAY EVEN HELP YOU.
HELP US? HOW?

JUST A MOMENT.
THERE! SEE! THAT'S A YOWIE. NOW JUST LOOK AT THE PRETTY YOWIE.
PRETTY YOWIE... PRETTY YOWIE... PRETTY YOWIE. KEEP LOOKING.

SUCKED IN!
TAP! TAP! TAP!

IT'S JUST A BLACK SCREEN.
I DON'T THINK IT'S EVEN TURNED ON.

OK THEY FELL FOR IT. NOW RUN FOR YOUR LIFE AND DON'T STOP NO MATTER...
WHAT!
HEY BUD, THE FUN'S BACK THAT WAY.
HOW'D HE GET IN FRONT OF ME?

YOU NOT GONNA FIND ANY FUN IN THAT DIRECTION MATE, BUT GOOD LUCK.
PERSONALLY I WOULDN'T GO THAT WAY IF I WERE YOU.
WHY THE HECK NOT?
THUMP!

I TOLD YA! DOESN'T LOOK LIKE FUN.
GURP!

JEEZ! WHERE'D HE COME FROM?
QUICK! INTO THE WATER.
WHOO! NOPE! BAD IDEA!
NAH, I WOULDN'T GO THERE EITHER MATE.
UP THE TREE! ASAP!

HHAAARRRKK
OH @#$%! MORE DINOSAURS!!
LOOK PAL, I DON'T WANT ANY TROUBLE.
WHERE HAVE ALL THE CUTE AND CUDDLY ANIMALS LIKE KANGAROOS GONE?
GETTING HOT, HOT, HOTTER!

BINGO!
CRUNCH!
OH, THEY DON'T LOOK HAPPY.
GGGRRR!
QUICK! GIVE THE CUTE & CUDDLY KANGAROO A HUG.
OH! WHAT NOW?
HHHSSSSSSS

AARRRHH!
I JUST STEPPED ON A SNAKE.
WHAT NEXT?
GRRR!
GRRR!
DINGOES! OF COURSE. WHAT'S A HORRIBLE WAY TO DIE IN THE OUTBACK WITHOUT DINGOES.

GRR!
HARK!
GRRR!
GRRR!
HISSSSS
HARK!
NAAR
HEY GUYS!... THIS ISN'T FUN AT ALL.

OK, LET'S EVEN IT UP A BIT.

SMACK!
SMACK!
TEEERRRR!
OW!
OW!
OW!
THUMP!
GGUUURRRKK!

WHO'S YOUR HERO?!

KA-BOOM!!!
MY MIND IS BLOWN, MAN!
THAT'S THE MOST AWESOME THING I'VE EVER SEEN! HOW'D YOU DO ANY OF THAT?
DO WHAT? WRESTLING? I'VE BEEN WRESTLING SINCE I WAS A FURBALL.
YOU'RE LIKE A BIG HAIRY CROCODILE DUNDEE.
WHO?
AH FORGET HIM! TELL ME SOMETHING! HOW'D YOU GET IN FRONT OF ME BACK THERE IN THE CAVE?
I USED A HAIRY HOLE... DON'T YOU KNOW WHAT A HAIRY HOLE IS?
NO! SHOW ME!

Three

THIS IS A HAIRY HOLE. THEY CAN TAKE YOU ANYWHERE YOU WANT.
INTERESTING.
CERTAINLY VERY HAIRY AS THE NAME SUGGESTS. HOW DO YOU USE IT?
IT'S EASY.
THUMP!
ARGH!

AAAAAAAAAAA
AAA
AAHR
AAAARHHA!!!
STOP WHINGING, SKINNY!

HAIRY HOLES (AS JOPLIN IS FINDING OUT)
ARE A VAST NETWORK OF FUR-COVERED TUNNELS THROUGHOUT THE OUTBACK'S UNDERGROUND. THEY CAN TRANSPORT A PERSON ANYWHERE IN THE RED CENTRE AT ANY TIME.

THE ONLY CATCH:
ONLY HAIRY HOLERS LIKE BEG AND RED KNOW WHERE THEY ARE AND HOW TO USE THEM.

'HINGS IN THE OUTBACK THAT WILL BLOW YOUR MIND!

THIS IS THE WORLD'S OLDEST CONTINUOUS DANCE PARTY. NO ONE KNOWS HOW LONG THE PARTY GOES BUT WE DO KNOW IT WAS THE FIRST PARTY & WILL PROBABLY BE THE LAST.
ALL ARE WELCOME AS LONG AS THEY ARE IN FAVOUR OF THE DJ'S FLAVOUR.

THE OUTBACK IS ALSO AN INTERGALACTIC PIT STOP FOR ALIEN FREIGHTERS. CRASH LANDINGS ARE VERY COMMON OUT HERE.
YIKES! THEY GOT A TOUGH JOB.
THE U
THE GALAXY
IT HAS

ANUS BLOSSOM.
MOST DANGEROUS PLANT.
UIT THAT BITES BACK.

O!M!G!
THIS HAS BEEN AWESOME!
THE POOP'N'CHOOP! THE DANCING, THE BITING & THE FIGHTING
ALL OF IT! JUST! WOW!
WHAT'S THE NEXT STOP, BEG?
BEGLEY.
HEY MATE, WHAT ARE YOU STARING AT?
WHAT'S GOT YOU SO STUMPED?
NO MATTER WHERE I GO OR WHAT I SEE.
THIS FREAKS ME OUT THE MOST.

THOSE TWO LITTLE HAIRY HOLES, YOU SEE THEM?
THAT'S WHERE RED AND I WERE BORN.
I DON'T UNDERSTAND. WHERE ARE YOUR PARENTS?
THEY HAD TO LEAVE US HERE. I WAS TOO YOUNG TO REMEMBER BUT RED STILL DOES.
I DON'T KNOW WHY THEY LEFT US BUT RED USED TO SAY THAT THEY'D COME BACK ONE DAY.
BUT THEY NEVER DID.

YOU MUST LOOK AFTER YOUR BROTHER, RED. NO MATTER WHAT!! WE'LL COME BACK ONE DAY. I PROMISE.
YOUNG RED & BABY BEG.
QUICK! WE NEED TO LEAVE THEM NOW! BEFORE THEY FIND ALL OF US.
WHEN RED REALISED THEY WEREN'T COMING BACK, THAT'S WHEN HE BECAME SUPER GRUMPY AND STARTED DRINKING GRUB TEA.

SO... YOU DON'T REMEMBER YOUR PARENTS?
NAH, NOT A THING.
SORRY I DIDN'T MEAN TO KILL THE MOOD. WE DON'T HAVE TO SEE THIS. IT'S A PRETTY BORING STORY.
TRUST ME, BEG. THERE'S NOTHING REMOTELY BORING ABOUT YOU.

THAT DOES IT! I'VE MADE UP MY MIND.
ABOUT WHAT?
I'M GOING TO HELP YOU FIND YOUR PARENTS.
HEHE, DID YOU DRINK SOME OF RED'S GRUB TEA?
I'VE CRAWLED & COMBED EVERY HAIRY HOLE IN THE OUTBACK. THEY AREN'T HERE.
BUT YOU HAVEN'T CHECKED THE REST OF THE WORLD.
THAT'S WHERE I COME IN.
I GOT A PLAN!

WHAT!
YOU OUTTA YA MIND?

Four

YOU WANNA GO OUT IN THAT WORLD? THAT WORLD FULLA SKINNIES?
CAN YOU NOT SAY THAT WORD IN FRONT OF JOE?
CRUNCH!
SNAP!
SMASH!
THAT'S OK. I LIKE IT. IT MAKES SENSE.
LISTEN, WE DON'T HAVE TO GO ANYWHERE.
THAT'S RIGHT! THAT'S THE BEAUTY OF HEADTWERK. IT BRINGS THE WORLD TO YOU.
WHAT DIJUN HEADTWERK?
IT'S THE SOCIAL MEDIA PLATFORM I CREATED. HERE, LET ME SHOW YOU ON MY LAPTOP.
STUBBOI! WE NOT FALLING FOR DAT ONE AGAIN.

I SWEAR I WILL NOT ESCAPE. (WELL, NOT YET)
WE JUST WANT YOU TO LOOK AT IT.
WHAT IF THERE WERE MORE HAIRY HOLERS OUT THERE? WHAT IF WE COULD FIND THEM?
WE'VE SEARCHED THE WHOLE BUSH AND FOUND... WHAT THE!
TOLD YA!

PROPER NASTY.
PROPER CREEPY
PLAIN UGLY.
THAT'S BESIDE THE POINT. DON'T YOU GET IT? THERE ARE MORE OF US OUT THERE. SURE, THEY'RE NOT AS GOOD LOOKING AS US BUT THIS IS OUR CHANCE TO FIND THEM.
TO FIND MUM AND DAD.
YARMMY!
YOU BOTH YARMMIES, GO AHEAD! WASTE YOUR OWN TIME LOOKING BUT DON'T COME CRYING TO ME WHEN YOU REALISE 'E GOT NO ONE OUT THERE TO CRY TO.

RED'S DAILY ROUTINE CONSISTS OF:
COLLECTING GRUBS.
SMASHING GRUBS.
PLUCKING PRICKLES FROM HIS BUTT HAIR.
ARGH! ANOTHER ONE!!!
DRINKING GRUB TEA AND SNOOZING.

THE NEXT MORNING
GOOD MORNING!
YOU BIN SCARE THE BUTT-SPIT OUT OF ME.
GOOD MORNING, BRO.
HE'S DONE IT!

I'VE DONE IT, BRO. BELIEVE IT OR NOT, I'VE DONE IT.
DONE WHAT?
HOME
WATCH
NOTICE
TAG
MESSAGE
I'VE TAKEN US ONLINE.
PROPABEGHOLE__02 ///h#
INFO
PHOTO
VIDEO
CHAT
EMOJI
HIS ROCK ELVIS PROFILE PIC HAS 50 LIKES ALREADY. NOW JUST WAIT FOR THE FRIEND REQUESTS TO ROLL IN.
WE JUST GOT TO STICK TO THE PLAN.
WHAT PLAN?

IT'S GENIUS. WE'RE GOING TO REACH OUT TO EVERY HAIRY HOLER, YOWIE, SASQUATCH, YETI, WILD MAN AND GET THEM ONLINE TO SHOW THE WORLD HOW COOL THEY ARE.
HOW ARE YOU PLANNING ON FINDING THAT MOB?
I'VE GOT MY OWN MILLION DOLLAR SATELLITE WATCHING EVERYTHING I DO.
HAHAHA! 'BIG DEADLY SATELLITE'. YOU STILL GOT LOST OUT HERE.
YES I GOT LOST BUT DOESN'T MEAN I COULDN'T BE FOUND.

THIS IS MY S.O.S. GPS BEACON. I CLICK THIS & MY PRIVATE HELICOPTER WILL BE HERE IN 3..2..1
CLICK!
VOOM!
CHOP!CHOP!CHOP!CHOP!CHOP!CHOP!
PREPARE FOR EXTRACTION!
CHOP!CHOP!CHOP!CHOP!CHOP!CHOP!CHOP!

I KNOW THERE'S SOMETHING SUPER SPECIAL ABOUT YOU, BEGLEY.
I KNEW IT THE MOMENT WE MET.
WE'LL STAY IN TOUCH, MATE.
HOW HE GONNA STAY IN TOUCH? THIS BLOKE DON'T EVEN OWN A LAPTOP!
HE DOES NOW!

I ORDERED IT FOR YOU WHILE YOU WERE GETTING PRICKLES OUT OF RED'S BUTT HAIR!
IT'S SOLAR POWERED & LINKED TO MY SATELLITE.
SEE YOU ON THE FLIPSIDE, AMIGO!
ON THE FLIPSIDE! AMIGO!

Five

SO THE JOURNEY INTO FINDING SOCIAL MEDIA MATES HAD BEGUN & ALL BEG COULD DO WAS WAIT...
I MADE GRUB BALLS! YOU WANT GRUB BALL?
SO HE WAITED...
I GOT 'NOTHER PRICKLE! HELP ME!
AND WAITED...
I'M RUNNING OUT OF EARWAX FOR DIS SCULPTURE. GIMME SOME EARWAX.

AND WAITED.
WHAT HAVE I DONE WRONG?
HUH!
I DON'T KNOW WHAT I'M DOING WRONG? I'VE GOT HUNDREDS OF PHOTO LIKES AND A FEW POST SHARES BUT NOT ONE SINGLE FRIEND REQUEST.
RELAX BRUZ, LET ME HAVE LOOK, AYE.

HERE, HAVE A GRUB BALL.
HMMM... HMMM... YEP.
MUNCH! MUNCH!
GGUURRKKK!!
BURRRRRR!
HMMM, I SEE.

THAT WAS SO GROSS!! WHAT WAS THAT?
SORRY BUD, THAT MIGHT NOT HAVE BEEN A GRUB BALL. MIGHT HAVE BEENA STINKBOMB I MADE EARLIER.
OK, I CHECKED AND I WORKED THE PROBLEM WITH YOUR PROFILE.
OH, THANKS RED.
SO WHAT'S THE PROBLEM? TELL ME STRAIGHT.
THE PROBLEM NOT DA PROFILE. DA PROBLEM IS YOU!

WHEN YOU GONNA FACE THE FACTS? WE MONSTERS.
THEY DON'T WANT TO BE FRIENDS WITH US.
THEY WANT TO STARE AT US LIKE FREAKS.
HE WAS USING YOU TO BLOW UP HIS OWN PROFILE.
BUT JOE WAS MY FRIEND. HE WAS A GOOD SKINNY.
NO SUCH THING AS A GOOD SKINNY. SKINNIES ARE ONLY GOOD FOR EATING. YOU KNOW WHY YOU DON'T HAVE ANY FRIEND REQUESTS?

SAME REASON MUM & DAD LEFT US... BECAUSE WE LOSERS!
SMACK!
BRO, YOU'RE A BIGGER LOSER FOR THINKING YOU CAN BE FRIENDS WITH THAT SKINNY.
LOSER!
THUD!

IS THAT...
YOU HAVE 1 FRIEND REQUEST
A FRIEND REQUEST? I GOT A FRIEND REQUEST!?

HEY REDLEY! I GOT A FRIEND REQUEST!
YARMY!
FRIEND REQUEST...MR... CRYPT...HUNTER_19! ACCEPT!
AND HE ALSO WROTE A MESSAGE!
Yo! propabeg_hole82 just wanted to say how aweome your pics are.
are they real?
hey Crypt-hunter19 yes my pics are 100% real.

what about you?
how do i know you re real and not some phony catfish??
im real, i swear. As real as you are.
how can i prove it?
LOL!!! chill out pal. just fooling with ya. but maybe we should meet and hang out?
absolutely!
would love to meet and hang out with you.
HOW WILL... I FIND... YOU?
TAP TAP TAP
TAP TAP
TAP TAP

OH DON'T YOU WORRY.
I'LL FIND YOU.
THINGS ARE GONNA GET KRAY-ZAY!
CLICK!
TO BE CONTINUED

Meanwhile... in the Hairy Hole...

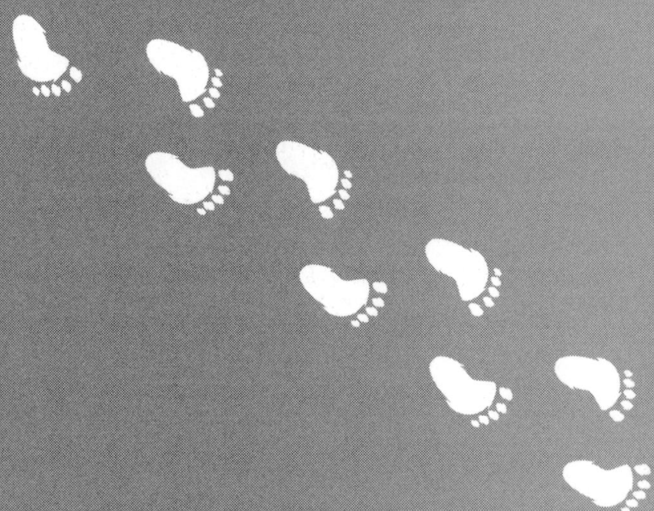

IT'S WRESTLE-KOALA-MANIA! IT'S MARSUPIAL FIGHT CLUB.

FINALS ARE NEXT WEEK IF YOU'RE STILL AROUND.

HOW TO DRAW A HAIRY HOLER!
1.
START WITH A CIRCLE.
2.
NOW DRAW 2 CIRCLES LIKE THIS WITH A LINE GOING DOWN THE MIDDLE.
3.
NOW DRAW A LINE ACROSS THE TOP OF THE BOTTOM CIRCLE. THAT'S WHERE WE PUT OUR NOSE.
HORNS
NOSE
4.
NOW WE DRAW FOREHEAD LINES, 2 CIRCLES FOR HORNS & A HAIRLINE.
5.
NOW DRAW YOUR FEATURES, NOSE, EYES, EARS, MOUTH, BROAD BROW.
6.
ONCE YOU'VE DONE YOUR FEATURES, YOU CAN ADD THE HAIRY STUFF & ANYTHING ELSE YOU WANT.

WHAT ARE THE HAIRY HOLES?

THE HAIRY HOLES ARE HAIR COVERED TUNNELS THAT CROSS AND INTERSECT EACH OTHER THROUGHOUT THE WHOLE OUTBACK UNDERGROUND.

THEY CAN TRANSPORT A PERSON ANYWHERE IN MERE SECONDS.

IF YOU EVER THOUGHT YOU SAW A HAIRY HOLER IN THE BUSH AND THEY JUST DISAPPEARED, CHANCES ARE THEY USED A NEARBY HAIRY HOLE FOR A QUICK GETAWAY.

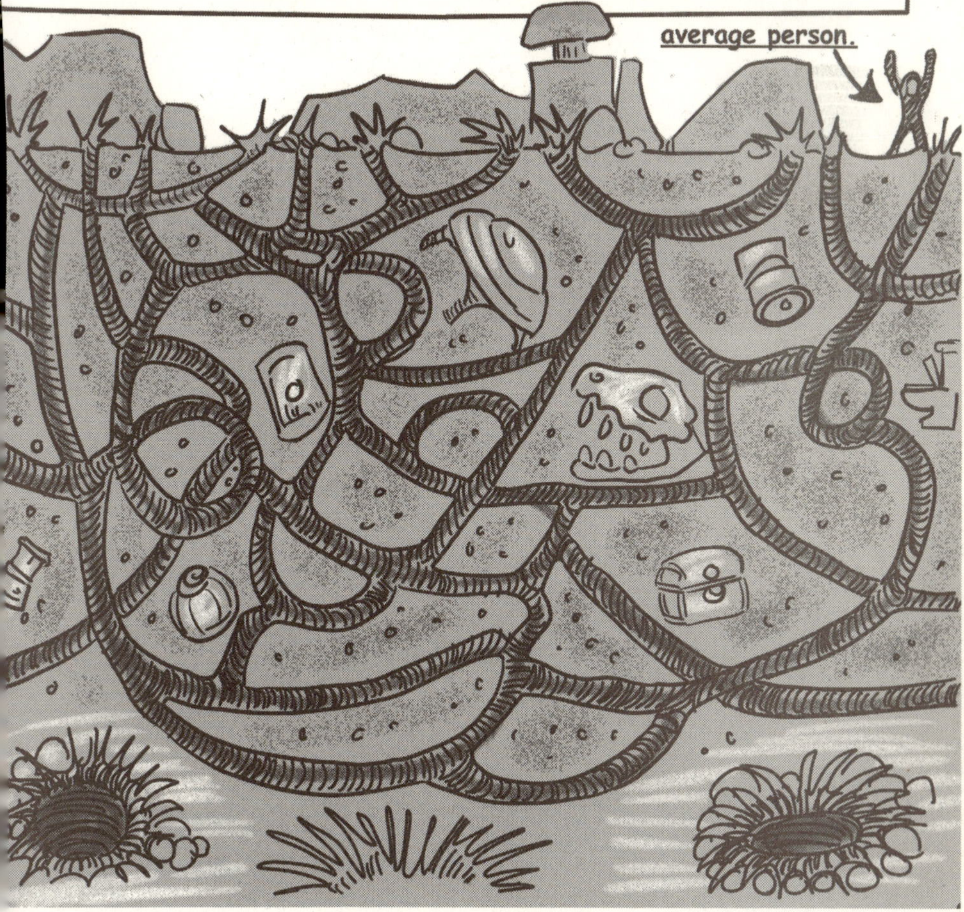